Ten Fun Things to
Do Before You Die

Ten Fun Things to Do Before You Die

BY NUN OTHER THAN
Karol Jackowski

HYPERION

NEW YORK

Library of Congress Cataloging-in-Publication Data

Jackowski, Karol.
    Ten fun things to do before you die / by nun other than
    Karol Jackowski.—1st ed.
        p. cm.
    Text partly revised.
    ISBN: 0-7868-8547-5
    1. Happiness. 2. Conduct of life. I. Title.
BJ1481.J23 2000
170'.44—dc21   99-047370

Designed by Ruth Lee

FIRST EDITION

10   9   8   7   6   5   4   3   2

THIS
BOOK
IS
DEDICATED
WITH
ENDLESS LOVE
TO MY
VERY
BEST FRIEND
IN THE
WHOLE WORLD

_____

ACKNOWLEDGMENTS

There are six degrees of separation between me and this book. First, there are three in one: the Sisters of the Holy Cross, Saint Mary's College, and Ave Maria Press, all neighbors in South Bend, Indiana. For twenty-five years, the sisters and the college gave me every kind of support a writer needs to sit down and make books. Ave Maria Press gave me every kind of support a writer needs to get her books published. Without the Holy Cross sisters, the students at Saint Mary's, Frank Cunningham and Ave Maria Press, this book would probably be nothing more than a great idea I had in 1987.

The second degree of separation between me and this book is my friend and sister (ex-nun) of thirty-five years, Linda Heidinger. When I moved to New York City in 1991 to finish a Ph.D. and write books, Linda gave me a day job helping manage Alphabets—her small chain of extraordinary New York toy and gift stores. While religion and retail at first seemed like an odd coupling, it ended up being a match made in heaven. Thanks to my sister Linda, I found all kinds of religious life in retail as well as everything I needed to write, including two rooms of my own in New York City.

It was through Linda also that I was introduced to Joan Stern, the third degree of separation between me and this book as well as the divine link to the fourth, fifth, and sixth—Susan Dalsimer at Miramax Books, Laurie Liss at the Harvey Klinger Agency, and Maureen O'Brien at Hyperion. Within one week—albeit Passover and Holy Week—those four wonder women made this book happen and gave me far more than I ever imagined as a writer. Only in New York.

For all the fun that's in this book, you have my most fun family and my very best friends to thank—especially my mother, Shirl, Queen of All Fun, and my dad, Henry, now resting in peace. Even before there were degrees of separation, and all along the way, family and friends consistently made me laugh and gave me the divine stuff to write about. Special heartfelt gratitude also goes to the Sisters for Christian Community. When it comes to being a nun, they are my daily inspiration.

All of the above had something divine to do with the making of this book. Without them I'd be speechless. I will acknowledge and thank them the rest of my life.

CONTENTS

Foreword   1

FIRST THING: Have More Fun Than Anyone Else   5

SECOND THING: Get Some Insight   16

THIRD THING: Get Some Depth   25

FOURTH THING: Find a Place to Escape Reality   35

FIFTH THING: Write Something at the End
                  of Every Day   49

SIXTH THING: Think About Nuns   59

SEVENTH THING: Make Yourself Interesting   82

EIGHTH THING: Live Alone for a While   93

NINTH THING: Treat Yourself   111

TENTH THING: Live Like You Have Nothing to Lose   116

Afterword   121

FOREWORD

In its original form, this book was a lecture given in the spring of 1987 at Saint Mary's College, Notre Dame, Indiana. As part of a student-planned program called "The Last Lecture Series," faculty and administrators were invited to prepare a lecture pretending it was the last one given before we died—our parting words. Because I was dean of students at the time, I suggested that the only reason they invited me was that they wanted me dead the next morning. I never underestimate the power of a drop-dead good lecture. But lecturing has never been a burning interest of mine, and it was difficult at first to imagine wanting to give one right before I died. I almost declined the invitation but decided instead to leave behind a list.

Making lists has always been a source of great fascination for me and obviously countless others (e.g., the Ten Commandments, "50 Ways to Leave Your Lover," the Seven Deadly Sins). The point-by-point appeal is universal. So making a list of all the things I'm real glad I did before I died, and all the things I suggest they think about doing before they die, is how this book got started. The list turned into the lecture, which felt like the outline for a book, the end result of which you are holding in your hands.

One thing to keep in mind about this particular list is that the items are not given in any order of importance. All are listed in the way they came to mind, and all are profoundly important at one time or another, some all the time. So don't be shocked to find that, for a nun, fun is number one on the list and God number three. All ten things connect. None stands alone or apart from the others.

Making your own list is a must. The experience itself is worth tons more than the price of this book. Plus you never know where your list will lead. "Ten More Things to Do Before You Die" has a nice ring to it, or "Ten Things to Never Do Before You Die": The possibilities are endless. For a real sweet treat, ask children to make a list. I asked my niece and nephews (ages seven, ten, and five at the time) what one thing they thought everybody should do before they die. Immediately and with great enthusiasm all three yelled, "Watch *G.L.O.W.* on Saturday night." *G.L.O.W.*—Gorgeous Ladies of Wrestling. Then came their list of favorite *G.L.O.W.* girls—Tina Ferrari, Mountain Fiji, Attache, Palestina, and Soul Patrol. My favorite was the tag team of Spike and Chainsaw. The possibilities are as fun as they are endless. Do make your own list.

TEN THINGS TO DO BEFORE I DIE

1. HAVE MORE FUN THAN ANYONE ELSE.
2.
3.
4.
5.
6.
7.
8.
9.
10.

Have More Fun Than Anyone Else

Having more fun than anyone else always comes to mind as the very first thing to do before you die. Fun—my favorite F word. Fooling around. Finding the good laugh waiting to be discovered. When it comes to having fun, I often feel as if few have had as much as I. Life has been jam-packed and fun-filled with divine experiences I never would've known had I not taken the strange, at the time funny-looking, less-traveled road of a nun. So important is that road to my having had so much fun that "Think About Nuns" ended up number six on my list of things to do before you die. The longer I lived the life of a nun, the richer, the holier, and the funnier my days became. That's its promise for women as well as its staying power for me.

Lest you think that all the emphasis on fun is little more than a silly tiptoe through the tulips, think again. Anyone who's funny knows there's a dear price to be paid for all the foolishness. Having more fun than anyone else means you always have to work twice as hard at everything for not being serious enough. And you are most likely to be taken less seriously as a result. But trust me on this one: It's always well worth the extra effort. Nothing refreshes, comforts, and heals like a good time. Nothing exhilarates and sends the soul soaring more than having the best time ever—so much so that face muscles ache from such hearty laughter. You must know that kind of fun often before you die. May you have millions of such laughs. Time rarely gets more divine than that.

With an infinite number of ways to have more fun than anyone else, it took me nearly half a century to find four.

Four Ways to Have Fun

1. Find fun people.

Oddly enough, one of the hardest things to find throughout this life is fun people. Far too few fill our days and nights, and seemingly fewer survive adulthood. I know it's not at all true that the older you get, the less there is to make you laugh. On the contrary, the older I get, the more there is that makes me laugh, and the less there is that bugs me or throws me for a loop. It's a fine art to have more fun when alone, and the pure joy of all that fun gets divinely multiplied and intensified by the company of other funny people. The time capsule in my mind is loaded with such precious moments, any one of which can set me off into laughing just as I did then. An amazing grace.

In the very serious search for fun people, these are some things to watch for: a good appetite, interesting work, good storytelling, slightly twisted sense of humor, fresh insight, brave choices. There are certainly other fun signs you know the minute you see them because they inspire instant laughter.

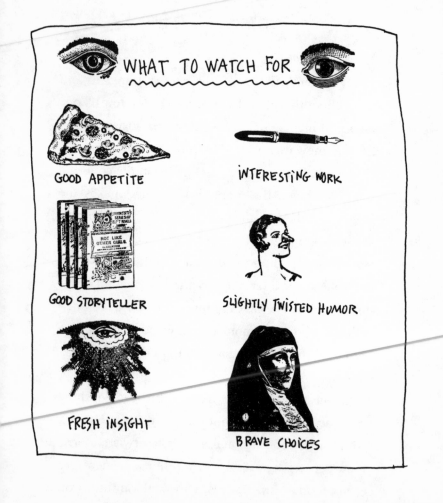

WHAT TO WATCH FOR

GOOD APPETITE

INTERESTING WORK

GOOD STORYTELLER

SLIGHTLY TWISTED HUMOR

FRESH INSIGHT

BRAVE CHOICES

Whoever discovered that "laughter is the best medicine" would undoubtedly agree that having so much fun is even good for your health. And finding people who always make you laugh is the surest guarantee for a happy and healthy life, now and forever. It's clearly one of the very best things you can do for yourself, and humankind, before you die.

2. Don't think about yourself around other people.

There are those in life who appear cursed with no desire at all to raise their attention and conversation above themselves. That is near irremediable. After about five minutes, it's also totally boring, dull, uninteresting, and monotonous. It even feels tiring and wearisome writing about it. Such selfishness is the stuff of which boredom is made, the number one killer of a good time. Left unchecked, it renders everyone incapable of having any fun at all, making it deadly enough to be a sin. The Eighth Deadly Sin.

A good general rule is to think about yourself when alone, and, when in the presence of others, think and ask about them. Expressing interest in the life and work of others not only leads to the delightful reputation of being an interesting person and good conversationalist, it also reveals immediately those with the greatest potential for fun. One thing you never want to do before you die is become a rude, boring, selfish, tiresome person. The secret lies in this: Forget about yourself around other people.

3. Be a fun person.

The only real foolproof way to have more fun than anyone else is for you yourself to become a fun person. Growing up in a funny family is certainly the most ideal training ground, with funny friends and relatives providing a great backup. The now-vintage experience of being taught by nuns in the 1950s is still an endearing source of laughter for many, as it was to my friends and me for years. Throughout life, it's very important to surround yourself with a majority who are fun to be with, including those we work for, live with, play with, hire, date, and marry. The fun ones always teach the importance of laughing at ourselves, a divine activity all its own as well as the heart and soul of growing up funny.

After all these years, I found two tried and true ways to stay funny. One is to make yourself interesting, and the other has to do with perfect timing. Making yourself interesting is so crucial to being funny that it turned up seventh on my list of things to do before you die, thus getting its own chapter. Suffice it to say now that each of us is endowed with a playful soul that always experiences as divine the most interesting and funniest of times. And the daily care and feeding of that playful soul is our holy duty until the day we die.

Perfect timing, carpe diem, is the soul mate of making yourself interesting and has everything to do with paying careful attention to the events of the day as they unfold, watching and waiting for moments loaded with potential for fun. There is no time with more divine potential for fun than the present moment. It passes once and never again. Now you see it. Now you don't.

So pay extra careful attention to the strange, disturbing, boring, moving, and hilarious parts of the day—the high-energy centers where potential for release and relief is greatest. Turn off the Pennsylvania Turnpike and visit Clyde Peeling's Reptile Farm. Never pass a Dairy Queen or Krispy Kreme without paying your respects. Take that mud

road back into a Louisiana bayou and watch your
whole life flash before you. Stop at every flea market
and garage sale. Go to the Coney Island Mermaid
Festival on the Summer Solstice. A funny person is
forever attentive to the present moment and rarely
fails to seize its divine opportunity for fun.

4. If it looks like fun and doesn't break the Ten Commandments, do it.

While talking about fun and the Ten
Commandments in the same sentence may sound
like a cruel joke, I still find both nowhere near as
foolish as they may appear. I also still find both
essential to my having more fun than anyone else.
Limitations, boundaries, comfort zones, knowing
when to stop, the point beyond which we do not go
without hurting or getting hurt. All are created
equal in order to keep us from destroying others
and ourselves in the endless pursuit of happiness.
Without a few basic guidelines for living happily
ever after, the capacity to get lost, seriously hurt, or
killed greatly magnifies.

However appealing it may appear, pursuing
unlimited possibilities does little more than over-

A SIGN FROM GOD

PENNSYLVANIA TURNPIKE

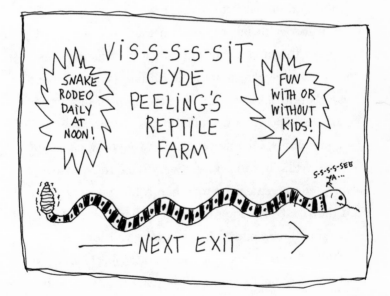

whelm us with countless experiences that always move faster than our conscious selves can keep up with. In due time, the juggling act falls apart and a spacey, confusing mindlessness becomes a way of life. Getting thrown off balance, we end up shifting priorities, consequently knowing ourselves and others less and less. Never a very pretty picture. Nothing funny about that at all.

In order to have more fun than anyone else, I suggest thinking about your own commandments, your own rules for living. "No hitting" is a good one, as is "Control your flock by keeping them in a large pasture." The Ten Commandments are probably the most famous, reliable set of rules we know, possibly this world's first to-do list. Every religion is divinely inspired to create rules for a happy life. So are we all. It didn't take me long to come up with Seven More Commandments, and it won't take you long either. While no one likes rules very much because they always appear to stand in the way of a very good time, you are not at all likely to have more fun than anyone else without them. So if it looks like fun and doesn't break the Ten Commandments, do it.

Second Thing:

Get
Some
Insight

The second thing to do before you die is get some insight. Without it you can never really have any fun at all. Without it you remain essentially clueless, eventually growing dumb and dumber. There is nothing worse than those with no insight. None more pitiable than the emperor with no clothes. Those who refuse to see never understand, and sometimes end up living mean, empty lives that are not even self-serving. Like dreams deferred, they all end up like raisins in the sun. This is the stuff of which horror movies are made. *The Blob. The Stepford Wives. The Living Dead.* That's how impor- tant it is to get some insight before you die. The consequences are absolutely pathetic, horrible, and too often deadly if you don't.

Insight is what you get when you look inside and get a glimpse, a clue as to what's going on. Always a breathtaking experience. Finding your best self and being that person is the end result of getting some insight. To be or not to be is always the question. If you don't find your best self, others will find many accommodating selves for you, often yielding sad, sometimes disastrous consequences.

Insight comes naturally to those who go through ordinary everyday life consistently trying to be their best self, the good twin. Always starting with wanting to be a better person, insight gradually grows deeper, moving you toward places of greater understanding, compassion, and fun. Because insight both saves and nourishes our soul, it's one of the most important things to get every day until we die. Nothing is worse than dying clueless, so don't mess around. Find and be your best self, now and forever.

Before you can get some insight, before you can see and hear what's going on within, you will most likely need some kind of peace and quiet in order to hear yourself think. As soon as possible, but most

definitely before you die, you must learn to love solitude and make it a part of your everyday life. There's
no getting insight without it. You may even learn, as
I did, to make solitude your lifestyle. Most mothers
(and nuns) I know purposely get up an hour or two
before everyone else because it's the only time for
peace and quiet they can find. After a long day out
or at work, I'll stay up half the night for the same
reason. Solitary splendor. If you haven't already
done so, you must discover solitude as the wellspring of insight it is, full of clues about what's
going on in your life and how fine you really are.

If you're wondering what to think about in solitude, start with your life and how pleased you are
with the way it's turning out. There's no better place
for getting insight than from the ordinary events of
everyday life. Begin also by making yet another list,
a Best Self List. Thinking about the best self you
want to be is always a good place to start getting
some insight. The starting point is always your self.
Your dear, sweet, mysterious self.

Now, you must be good and do good in order to
feel good. And the more specific you are about how
good you want to be, the greater the potential for

GO TO YOUR ROOM

THE
SOLE CAUSE
OF OUR
UNHAPPINESS
IS THAT
WE DO NOT
KNOW HOW
TO STAY QUIETLY
IN OUR ROOM.

- PASCAL

insight. For example, wanting to be a "nice person" isn't quite as insightful and helpful as wanting to be less judgmental of those who do things you don't agree with. In making your Best Self List, you are always totally free to create the best self you want. Think of it as your Personal Top Ten, a high holy list. A Worst Self List is just as helpful, just as loaded with divine insight, and just as much a high holy list.

Once you've completed the Best Self List, check it with your life to see how close you are to being all that you can be. Do the same with the Worst Self List. In doing so, pay careful attention to the most moving parts of your day, circumstances that make you happy, sad, mad, overwhelmed, confused, surprised. Whatever moves you bears divine insight. For believers it occasionally feels like a cosmic little tap or poke from Gods or angels—sometimes playful, sometimes like a sock in the nose, sometimes like a still, small voice—always divine.

There's a heap of divine insight to be found in the ordinary manner of our days. Always pay special attention to those people, events, and choices that bring out the best and the worst in you, the good twin or the evil twin. Your gut feeling will let you know how well you're doing and will nag you with crabbiness until you get the message—the clue you need to "see more clearly, love more dearly, follow more nearly."

For those who have the eyes to see, insight always comes from the best and worst parts of any given day. The Gods have just as much to say when good things happen to good people as they do when bad things happen to good people and when both things happen to bad people. Good news and bad news both bear divine insight. The sun shines on good and bad alike.

Three months before I entered the convent, at my high school graduation, I was given a holy card from a nun that said "God writes straight with crooked lines." At first I wondered if she maybe thought my joining the convent was one of God's crooked lines. My lingering thought though is how godlike we all are in that respect. We too write straight with crooked lines. By the grace of that God all disappointments, failures, mistakes, even tragedies become part of the winding path of our lives, given as turning points, and loaded with divine insight— should we care and have the strength to see.

The best and happiest of times are no less insightful just because they feel so good. During the very best of times our primary job is to become grateful, humble, and generous. Then we can party hearty and wild. Thank God goodness is so tangible we can feel it. But the kind of thanks the Gods really love are those that move us to be kind, just, forgiving, and generous. Nothing pleases the Gods more than the sight of global sharing. If you're not in that picture, I suggest you do something about it before you die. Share share share.

What we do with what we get is always loaded with divine insight. It's also the stuff of which final judgments are made. And it's in everyone's best interest to pay undivided attention to every bit of it, especially those insights that lead us to discover what enough is. It's a pity so few in this world find it. Don't be one of them. Get as much insight as you can before you die. As far as the Gods are concerned, it's the one thing we can never get enough of. And as far as we're concerned, it's the one thing we can never get enough of without getting fat. Insight is 100 percent fat free. Good for the heart.

↑

INSIGHT: 0 CALORIES

Third Thing:

Get
Some
Depth

If you're having more fun than anyone else and getting some insight, it won't be long before you begin to acquire some depth. While insight strengthens the life of our heart, depth does the same for the life of our soul. It takes us well below the surface of events, as below as we want to go, to the deepest, inmost part of our soul—the holy of holies. Depth is a big goal for all believers, because life as we know it makes no sense without it. Without it we're all lost souls, left to wander as we wonder if that's all there is.

While with insight we find our very best self, with depth we find our very best God. Eventually

wisdom comes, embraces us, and shows us both
are really one and the same. Human life is so
sacred that most of us cannot help but believe
that some God must have had a hand in making us
and some God must still have a hand in keeping
us alive. Every religion, from the most primitive to
the most contemporary, is founded on the belief
that keeping in touch with that God is an inborn
necessity—like the air we breathe.

The only way to get some depth, to get ready
to meet your Maker, is to start digging. Go beyond
the obvious to the heart of the matter and try to
see the hidden influences at work. Follow the advice
of the poet Rilke: "Go into your self and see how deep
the place is from which your life flows." You will
most likely find your best and worst self there. Good
twin and evil twin side by side. Stop, look, and listen.

The Upanishads found that the Gods love the
obscure and hate the obvious. There's always far
more than at first meets the eye, and it's there that
the Gods tend to hide and abide. It's there also that
you'll get some depth. Anytime there's oppression,
misery, death, sin, or trouble in River City, the Gods
hear those prayers and begin to stir. Believers often

find that when life gets intense, so does the inner activity of God—sometimes intensely near, sometimes intensely far, sometimes intensely silent, sometimes bestowing incredible excesses of strength, sometimes nada nada nada.

All of this goes to show that our very best God is likely to be found in the unknown, unseen, undone parts of life. The parts of life that hurt and make us sick and tired, those are the places to start digging. Dig also in those places where you've been taken to the limit as well as those that lie motionless and at a standstill. The land of the soul is an open field for digging, and any sign of disturbing activity or suspicious inactivity is a big clue about where to start. It's the "X" that marks the spot. There are more divine treasures than you can imagine buried in our soulful fields, all just waiting to be discovered.

You can take great comfort now in knowing that after a while, everything that happens to you, everything you dig up, even all the dirt, becomes exceedingly precious and simply divine. Strange but true. Strange because it doesn't readily make sense, but true because the deeper you go, the closer you get,

and the closer you get, the more peaceful and inde-structible you become. Being more firmly grounded, and having acquired considerable depth, you are no longer so easily thrown or confused by the fickle fin-ger of fate, not so easily paralyzed or disturbed by cir-cumstances beyond your control; you are centered.

While knowing where to dig for depth is the first step to getting some, recognizing a good God when you find one is quite another matter, and oddly enough sometimes far more difficult. Here are two more lists, checklists to help you recognize good Gods. If your God does and does not do the things on the list, blessed are you. You hit paydirt. Welcome to the Magic Kingdom. If not, blessed are you too—but I strongly suggest you keep digging.

A Word About Nonbelievers

One of the most unattractive features of some believers is the mindless tendency to be sinfully judgmental of nonbelievers. Without their God, they think nonbelievers must be hopeless, empty, and evil. In the eye of the beholder, I say. Einstein was a self-proclaimed nonbeliever whose experience of

SEVEN THINGS A GOOD GOD WILL DO

- ☐ MAKE YOU WAIT.
- ☐ CALM FEARS.
- ☐ SHOW NEXT STEPS.
- ☐ MAKE YOU LAUGH OR BLINK.
- ☐ GET YOU THROUGH.
- ☐ KEEP LIFE INTERESTING.
- ☐ SET YOU FREE.

I LIKE IT.

SEVEN THINGS A GOOD GOD WON'T DO

- ☐ TAKE PAIN AWAY.
- ☐ KILL OR HIT.
- ☐ GIVE UP.
- ☐ BORE YOU OR WASTE YOUR TIME.
- ☐ LIE, CHEAT, OR STEAL.
- ☐ LEAVE YOU ALONE.
- ☐ WHATEVER YOU WANT.

I WANT IT.

life, he says, was profoundly religious, as are all his writings—he being one of millions like him in that regard.

Most nonbelievers I know are those who find that life itself is divine and that's religion enough. Others have reason to believe life is not divine, this is all there is, and ours is only to deal with what we get dealt. I suspect some nonbelievers have never known what a good God can do and find it hard to believe it's good for humankind that such a God exists. Nonbelievers I know have no desire at all for the Gods of religion, finding the mere thought of one oppressive. Believing that all Gods are made in our own image and likeness, nonbelievers find that such divinity warrants nothing but profound disbelief.

Before religion got organized, faith in God meant trusting your intuition, your gut instinct, as divine. It meant always letting conscience be your guide. For believers, the whole world was charged with the grandeur of Gods and all of life was sacred. Those were the good old days. With the universe as temple, the true nonbeliever, much like the true believer, finds as many ways to truth as there are moments in a day, all bearing divine life. Nonbelievers tend to know mostly what a good God doesn't do, and believers tend to know mostly what a good God does do. The truth of the matter is that neither lies very far from the other. Both stand back to back, sometimes side by side, making a delicate balance.

Fourth Thing:

Find a Place to Escape Reality

Seen by some as one of the first signs of mental illness, escaping reality is clearly one of the best things I ever learned to do before I die; so much so it feels like I was born knowing how, like I inherited an Escape gene. Many think that being a nun is one of the greatest escapes of all, and in a very good way it most certainly is. It's the only way some of us know not to lose sight of what's real. But other than that, the joys and struggles of life are not much different for nuns than they are for anyone else. Human nature is what it is no matter who you are or how you live. A rose is a rose is a rose.

Knowing limits or being pushed to the ends of

them is all it takes to set off the need to escape reality. Whenever I feel confused, overwhelmed, overloaded, over anything, I always head for the hills. Hit the Escape key and go. Too much of anything—including tequila—will do it. Enough is enough, and no one knows better than you do when you've reached or gone past your limit. So when you find you've had enough, take leave, escape as soon as you can, and don't come back until you have to.

Before you die you must find and cultivate great escapes, places inside and out where you can easily get away from it all; places that are naturally mind altering. Inside places have always been my greatest escapes, and a room of my own, paradise. Never having had much access to the world of great outside escapes, the inner world easily became wonderland for me. A virtual theme park. From the moment I was born, imagination was my Siamese twin. And thanks to my parents we were never separated at birth. Now I know that imagination is everyone's inborn place to escape reality. William Blake called it "the divine body in everyone." Others find in imagination the workshop of the Gods and their Muses, an interior castle of divine creative powers. Heaven on earth.

ESCAPE REALITY

BY JANE WAGNER

REALITY IS THE LEADING CAUSE OF STRESS
AMONGST THOSE IN TOUCH WITH IT.
I CAN TAKE IT IN SMALL DOSES,
BUT AS A LIFESTYLE,
I FOUND IT TOO CONFINING.
IT WAS JUST TOO NEEDFUL;
IT EXPECTED ME TO BE THERE FOR IT
ALL THE TIME,
AND WITH ALL I HAVE TO DO--
I HAD TO LET SOMETHING GO.
NOW,
SINCE I PUT REALITY ON A BACKBURNER,
MY DAYS ARE JAM-PACKED
AND FUN-FILLED,

The daily care and feeding of imagination is just as important to do before you die as is that of the body, heart, and soul. There's so little real fun in life without it. The divine body in me always has a taste for reading, writing, and loafing—doing nothing. Give me a good book, paper and pen, solitary splendor, and I'm gone. Superior devotion to reading, I find, is a sure way to cultivate and feed the imagination. There's nothing quite like getting a good book and wallowing around in someone else's world for a while. There's also nothing like newspapers and magazines to give perspective to your days and you the ability to see things in true relationship.

So holy was reading to the formation of a nun that hours were reserved every day for the exclusive activity of "lectio divina," spiritual reading, snacktime for the divine body. If you haven't done so already, begin right now to cultivate a deep love for reading. Be sure to set aside some time every day for lectio divina and don't stop doing so until you die. Read. Read. Read. Lectio divina is so important that it should become a rule of life, period.

A superior devotion to reading often leads to imagination's other best friend, writing—or any

LECTIO DIVINA

A
POEM
BY
EMILY
DICKINSON
→

A WORD IS DEAD
WHEN IT IS SAID,
SOME SAY.

I SAY IT JUST
BEGINS TO LIVE
THAT DAY.

#1212

other kind of soulful activity. Writing is so vital to the life of my imagination that it ended up fifth on the list of things to do before you die. For others it could be painting, gardening, coloring, acting, raising a family, cooking, building, whatever. Find the art, craft, or hobby that best soothes and fills your soul and escape there as much as you can.

While it may be sad but true that we can't have our bread and loaf too, never let that be a reason to abandon the creative life completely. None of us lives by bread alone. And the imagination desperately and daily needs to loaf, do nothing, waste time. Such leisure has always been the basis of art and culture, and it's our grave personal responsibility to see that it remains so. For Gertrude Stein it took "a heap of loafing" to write a new book. I do all of my reading and writing in bed. That's how important such blatant inactivity is to the life and work of the imagination.

All of the sitting around doing nothing allows the Gods and Muses to intervene and inspire without interference. Divine inspiration often comes when least expected, in the middle of doing absolutely nothing, sometimes even while sleeping.

Wasting time, loafing around, and doing nothing are some of the greatest and freest escapes I know. You too must become well practiced in all three before you die. May we all have days like the Queen in Alice's Wonderland who sometimes believed as many as six impossible things before breakfast.

Another great do-nothing escape made divinely mandatory by Mother Nature is sleep. And naps. To this day, I still look forward to falling asleep every night. And still treasure the rare day that I get a midafternoon nap. What goes on when we sleep remains one glorious mystery. Through the night, true rest refreshes the weary and sometimes heals the sick. Oftentimes problems get resolved, books get titles, confusion clears. And every night, whether we remember or not, we dream.

Sleep is just as mysterious as it is necessary, and much of the mystery has to do with how Gods traditionally visit believers in their sleep and through their dreams. Sleep has long been regarded as prime time for the Gods to do their work. Times of total unconsciousness are most favorable for divine activity due to the lack of human interference. Something altogether divine and mysterious happens when we sleep, making it the best mandatory escape from reality we have. If the Catholic Church were to add to its list of sacraments, sleep would be my recommendation for number eight. Just like sacraments, sleep can transform you, offering what's needed to wake up refreshed, rise from the bed, and make your way into a brand-new day.

Now, when it comes to great outside escapes, I know of two that I highly recommend doing frequently before you die, retreat and travel. Very early on in Catholic schools, we learned the importance of retreats, experienced mostly as a day or two off from school and homework. And a movie about being nuns and priests. Only much later did I find out how important, even critical, such retreats would be to the care and feeding of my body, heart, and soul.

Monthly and annual retreats were a very important part of our early training as nuns. One day a month, usually the first Sunday, was spent in silent retreat as well as an extended period annually, most often one or two weeks in the summer. The ancient practice of monthly and annual retreats among nuns continues to this day. That's how tried and true it is. We can't live without it.

SLEEP

BY
CHARLES PEGÚY

GOD SPEAKS:

I DON'T LIKE THE ONE WHO DOESN'T SLEEP, SAYS GOD.
I AM TALKING ABOUT THOSE WHO WORK AND DON'T SLEEP.
I PITY THEM. I HAVE IT AGAINST THEM. A LITTLE.
THEY WON'T TRUST ME.
THEY HAVE THE COURAGE TO WORK.
THEY LACK THE COURAGE TO BE IDLE,
TO STRETCH OUT. TO REST. TO SLEEP,
POOR PEOPLE, THEY DON'T KNOW WHAT'S GOOD.
THOSE WHO DON'T SLEEP ARE UNFAITHFUL TO HOPE.
THEY LOOK AFTER THEIR BUSINESS VERY WELL DURING THE DAY.
BUT THEY HAVEN'T ENOUGH CONFIDENCE IN ME
TO LET ME LOOK AFTER IT DURING THE NIGHT,
AS IF I WASN'T CAPABLE OF LOOKING AFTER IT
DURING ONE NIGHT.
HUMAN WISDOM SAYS,
DON'T PUT OFF UNTIL TOMORROW
WHAT CAN BE DONE THE VERY SAME DAY.
AND I TELL YOU:
PUT OFF UNTIL TOMORROW
THOSE WORRIES AND THOSE TROUBLES GNAWING AT YOU TODAY...
PUT OFF UNTIL TOMORROW
THOSE TEARS WHICH FILL YOUR EYES AND YOUR HEAD,
FLOODING YOU, ROLLING DOWN YOUR CHEEKS,
THOSE TEARS WHICH STREAM DOWN YOUR CHEEKS,
BECAUSE BETWEEN NOW AND TOMORROW, MAYBE I, GOD,
WILL HAVE PASSED YOUR WAY.
BLESSED IS THE ONE WHO PUTS OFF UNTIL TOMORROW.
THAT IS TO SAY, BLESSED IS THE ONE WHO HOPES,
AND WHO SLEEPS.

At first I could hardly tell the difference between retreat days and regular nun days, except that retreat days clearly felt like days off—slept later, no classes, no housework, no scheduled activities, and naps were allowed. Eventually I discovered how absolutely important it is to take days off like that regularly in order to prevent exhaustion and wearing yourself out. When life begins to irritate you and push you too close to the edge, the thing to do is retreat. Time out. Take a sick day if you have to. Do whatever you need to do to collect yourself and pull yourself together. Do whatever you need to do to retreat for a while.

You can even take a moment to retreat if need be. Go out for a walk, take a breather, cordially escape, and let that be the heartfelt prayer that it is. A source of great inner strength, retreating always allows us just enough time to catch our breath—then it lifts us up, gets us through, and returns us back to life feeling pretty brand new. Try it. You can't help but like it.

While I have not yet done much in the way of travel, I do know for sure that travel works much the same magic on the body and soul as does a good retreat. What more obvious way to escape reality than to take leave of where you are and go somewhere else? Wherever I go for retreat or travel, I always look for water, lakes, big bathtubs, oceans, and hot tubs. Nothing comforts, soothes, cleanses, and refreshes the weary body and soul like clear cool or hot water. Favorite spots, like all the old familiar places, offer a safe, secure, trustworthy escape. New spots—like places you've never been before, places you've never seen—offer an escape that's more exciting, challenging, and stimulating. Both have miraculous rejuvenating powers.

The third great escape, exercise, is one of which I know nothing but would nonetheless recommend highly. When it comes to any kind of exercise (except for running to the fridge during commercials), I really do not know whereof I speak. As a firm believer in never running unless someone is chasing me, and never buying shoes I have to bend over to tie, I have never found exercise to be a great escape. It only makes me hungry, thirsty, crabby, and achy. When it comes to no gain without pain, I'm simply not interested in working up the sweat. I hate to sweat and can't even envision wanting to.

Ever. There's enough sweat and pain in life just as it is. So I always ask why, why inflict more on yourself and sometimes others?

For the rest of the world, however, exercise is one of the healthiest ways to relieve stress and escape reality. Doctors and health experts everywhere agree that we won't live as long without it. Guess that answers my question. Even so, I'm still sitting on the sidelines, munching chips and chocolate, taking my chances. But the world is loaded with those whose bodies and souls are consistently refreshed and strengthened by aerobics, marathons, biking, jogging, power walking, pumping iron, and getting bruised and broken in contact sports. While all of the above fall into the category of things that clearly surpass my understanding, many do find exercise a tried and true way to escape reality. I remain unconvinced, overweight, and pray (never diet) daily to become thinner.

DIETER'S PRAYER

LOVELY LADY
DRESSED IN BLUE,
MAKE ME TALL
AND SKINNY,
JUST LIKE YOU.

SISTER MAURICE

Fifth Thing:

Write Something at the End of Every Day

For most, writing something at the end of every day would be one big waste of space on a list of things to do before you die. Most hate to write and are so tired at the end of the day that all they want is to be left alone with a cold drink, a good dinner, a hot tub—a nice relaxing evening alone, or with family and friends. While writing probably will never make your list of things to do before you die, I recommend that you think about it anyhow. It's the least you can do. Just for a moment, consider why you should write every day, what there is to write about, and what's so special about the end of the day.

My needing to write every day had absolutely

everything to do with the very first lesson we learned as new nuns on day one: the extraordinary importance of silence, of not talking. I suppose, practically speaking, with fifty eighteen- to twenty-one-year-olds living together, "no talking" had to be rule number one in order to preserve everyone's sanity. As the rule book wisely noted: "Conversational powers are no common gift, especially among women meeting daily in the same circle."

To its credit, the no-talking rule not only protected our soulful right to peace and quiet, but it also provided a distraction-free atmosphere in which to focus, concentrate, and do our work. No small blessing there. Every day I thank the Gods that honking horns, barking dogs, jackhammers, car alarms, motorcycles, and sirens do not disturb my work. Never underestimate the power to focus and concentrate. It's magic.

I never knew why or how writing could be so important until I learned about the no-talking rule and found that writing was the only way I could talk whenever I wanted. Writing always came to the rescue when I had to keep silent, and thereby became one of the greatest and most divine comforts I knew.

What I couldn't say out loud I could always say in a note, letter, or journal first. And whenever I felt totally speechless, writing always allowed me to find the necessary words. Listening to the writing voice didn't really happen seriously until I entered the convent and couldn't talk whenever I wanted. From that day forward I came to know and love the writing voice as divine. And from this day forward I wish the very same for you.

Particularly great was the rule of silence imposed on the end of the day, which was to be especially observed. It was even called the Great Silence or Grand Silence, indicating clearly that there was something great, grand, and mysterious about keeping quiet at night. According to monastic tradition, Great Silence began with the close of evening recreation (around 7:30 to 8:00 P.M.) and lasted until after Mass and meditation the next morning (around 7:30 to 8:00 A.M.)—nearly coinciding with what many believe are the psychic hours of 9:00 P.M. to 6:00 A.M. When the ordinary silence of the day turned Great, even eye contact counted as talking. That's how seriously holy silence was at night.

At first, I used to think the Great Silence rule was made up to keep monks and nuns from complaining at the end of the day. While many were indeed so tired they could hardly speak, some of us, the night people, were so wound up we could hardly sleep. Unfortunately, silence without is no guarantee of silence within. Being wrapped in the Great Silence either knocked you out and left you to rest in peace, or kept you awake because all you could hear was yourself think. That's when not being able to talk nearly killed me. That's when I started writing. And that's when the end of every day became highly and holy important.

What to write never presents much of a problem if you can hear yourself think. That's the ticket. And nothing amplifies the opportunity to hear yourself think more than some Great Silence at the end of the day. Try it. Start by writing about what everyday life offers you. Whenever the day feels done and you are settling in for the night, sit somewhere greatly silent and rerun the day like a movie in your mind. Then make lists. Two of them. While watching a movie of the day with your mind's eye, make a list of the Best Parts of the Day and the Worst Parts of the

Day. Then recalling what you did with both, elaborate.

Now when it comes to describing what you loved about the best parts of the day and hated about the worst parts, spare no detail. Be sure to include any other unusual or interesting parts of the day worth noting, like strange coincidences, letters received, close encounters, ticket stubs and Playbills, Chinese cookie fortunes, UFO sightings, whatever. Anything that distinguishes one day from all other days is always well worth noting in the end. It's all the stuff that makes up our Book of Days. Think of how rich and wise this world would be if everyone left behind a Book of Days.

Letters too are best written at night. Nighttime is divinely and naturally "Dear You . . ." time. Whenever the outside world quiets down, the inner voices are always much easier to hear, with thoughts and visions of loved ones more likely to appear. That's prime time for letter writing. Good old-fashioned letter writing with paper, pen, and an envelope sealed with a kiss, stamped with a commemorative, and sent on its way via U.S. mail.

The importance of writing at the end of every

A LETTER
IS A JOY
OF
EARTH —
IT IS
DENIED
THE
GODS.

#1639
EMILY DICKINSON

day grew gradually and oddly enough had everything to do with New Year's Eve, a high holy retreat
day for nuns. Being the least scheduled of all
retreats, New Year's Eve topped my list of Favorite
Retreat Days. Except for meals and a few communal
prayers, the day was pretty much your own. Big
chunks of unscheduled time. Even for naps.
Solemnly retreating on New Year's Eve also felt like
a purely contrary and outrageous way to celebrate
the New Year, always enhancing its significance.

The very best part of retreat days always was,
still is, and always will be the free time to do as you
please, to go where the Spirit leads or stays. A day to
attend solely to the Gods and their Muses. For me,
those huge chunks of retreat time provided hour
upon solitary hour for reading through all the daily
lists of bests and worsts and conducting "The Best
and the Worst of the Month Review." Then on New
Year's Eve, "The Annual Best and Worst of the Year
Awards." What a gala event that is.

I still do monthly reviews regularly and the
annual Best and Worst Awards at the beginning of
every New Year. After nearly twenty-five years of writing at the end of every day, I'm now working toward

the Best and Worst of a Lifetime. Both the monthly and annual reviews are tremendously insightful and entertaining spiritual exercises, mostly because there are few things more stunning and funny than seeing yourself and others in perspective. I also enjoy the rare and strange pleasure in knowing that I can pretty much pick any day over the past twenty-five years, pull out the book for that day, and see what happened. Like time traveling back through past lives. A trip that you too can take if you write every day.

Of course, the more faithful you are to the daily spiritual exercise of writing, the more insightful and enjoyable the monthly and annual reviews. That's why writing at the end of every day is so important. It's such good reading material for monthly and annual retreats. And its subtle ability to enhance our consciousness of daily events should never be underestimated. You are far more likely to be attentive to the current events of your day if you know you need to write something about the best and worst of them at night. Writing something at the end of the day is also the only way the habit of doing so can be acquired. And nun or not, this is one habit well worth acquiring before you die.

EVERY WORD BORN

OF AN INNER NECESSITY

WRITING MUST NEVER BE ANYTHING ELSE.

ETTY HILLESUM

Sixth Thing:

Think About Nuns

By far, one of the best things I ever did before I die is decide to be a nun. In one way it's not at all surprising. Spending at least eight hours a day with nuns from grade school through high school, it was hard not to think about them and how they lived. Those of us who grew up in Catholic schools before the late 1960s spent more of our waking hours with nuns than we did with our own families. They were our teachers, our mentors, our spiritual directors, our disciplinarians, our older sisters, and oftentimes our friends. So whether you actually became a nun or not, thinking and talking about them was something we did nearly every day for years. Even now, nuns rank right up there on the list of the Most Influential People in My Life.

Those who never grew up around nuns also can't seem to help but wonder what a nun is and why any woman would want to be one. The hidden mysteries of religious sisterhood remain a source of fascination and interest to many. Believer and nonbeliever alike, male as well as female, dear friend and near stranger, each want to know why I became a nun and why I still want to be one. In general, they question why any woman in her right mind would ever want to be a nun, particularly in this day, age, and country where a woman can pretty much be anything she wants.

Because of its universal appeal, and because I'm so glad I did it before I die, I strongly suggest that you too think seriously about nuns. Whether you can become a nun is neither here nor there. While you may have no chance at all of ever being a nun, there are still parts of the life that can and should be lived by everyone, men included. So don't you dare skip this chapter. And three ruler whacks on the knuckles if you do.

Even after a twelve-year association with nuns, I

thought far more about being one after I entered the convent than before. Then I really had something to think about. At age eighteen, all I knew about being a nun was that it mostly meant none of this and none of that and I got picked to be one. I also took serious notice of some nuns in high school who were very smart, very well traveled, and did very good work (and late at night). Most important, they always looked like they were having a lot of fun, totally enjoying the pleasure of one another's company. They were the kind of sisters I always felt very lucky to have.

Other than that, the hidden life of a nun was one big mysterious, well-guarded secret. And even after I entered the convent, it was only revealed bit by bit. Good thing. Wise women. If everything were revealed all at once, it would've been way too much—probably no one would join and no one would stay. Most likely we would never do anything important if we knew ahead of time all we'd have to go through. Bit by bit is all we can ever handle reasonably. When events unfold gradually like that, there's nothing to be afraid of. Anything more than bit by bit tends to overwhelm and frighten us, especially when it comes to life's great mysteries.

Mostly it was the strange, mysterious, other-worldly dimension of a nun's life that held the big attraction for me. The cares of a nun were quite clearly not of this world. Something totally beyond my understanding attracted me to those plain-looking women, living together on the fringe of society, doing brave and interesting work. Everything they did gave strong evidence of having discovered some deep, dark secret to life that had a lot to do with God—and a God who seemed fun to be with.

The most mysterious part of a nun's life always was and always will be "the call." The most mysterious part of everyone's life is always what they're called to be and do. There is not now nor has there ever been anything unusually dramatic or noteworthy about the call I heard—no visions, no extraordinary signs, stories, afflictions, or miracles. Nor did I come from a religiously observant family that always prayed and wished for one of their five children to become a nun or a priest. Quite the contrary. From all outward appearances there were no indications whatsoever that I'd get picked to be a nun. And if there had been a vote at the time, I easily would've been elected "Least Likely . . ." by my classmates.

ONE
NEVER GOES
SO FAR
AS WHEN
ONE DOESN'T KNOW
WHERE
ONE IS GOING.

GOETHE

From the very start, I recognized the call simply as a voice—a kind of hunch, an intuitive gut instinct. And by that voice I gradually knew what to do and where to go next. In time it felt like a divining rod, showing my thirsty soul where to find water. I also discovered gradually that I had a mind—a voice of my own—and another mind, as if my mind also had a mind of its own, with a more thoughtful, insightful voice. Together they grew to be the conscience I've always known and loved as guide, the voice I've always known and loved as divine.

Truth be told, all I really truly knew when I felt called to be a nun was this surprising need, a growing impulse to follow my uninformed, naïve fascination with those veiled women, to yield to the mysteriousness of it all, even leave family and friends for the sake of it. At the time I vaguely knew that when anything stirs us that deeply, moves us to the point of distraction, and urgently invites us to follow, we must pack up, go, and be not afraid. Never fear the less-traveled road. Respect such mysterious calls always and take them very seriously. Never ever minimize or regard them as foolishness.

In the beginning I blindly believed and trusted, but now I know and see for sure that such is the call of the Gods.

Equal in mystery to "the call" and equally as strange at first was the unusual lifestyle of nuns. They dressed differently, lived together, prayed a lot, worked hard, and believed extraordinary things. All the reasons I found to be a nun have to do with three things nuns believe that the rest of the world mostly doesn't. Even if there's absolutely no chance you could ever be a nun, these are well worth thinking about anyhow before you die—especially if you're interested in discovering some secrets to everlasting life.

Three Good Reasons to Live Like a Nun

1. All are treated equal.

The very first thing I noticed about nuns was how all were treated equal. The sisters who cooked and cleaned and did laundry were cherished members of the community just as much as the sisters who ran the schools and administered the hospitals. And those who ran the schools and hospitals also did their fair share of the cooking, cleaning, and laundry. Members form only one class. All enjoy the same rights and privileges, all work, and all are taken care of until the day they die. Freedom from daily worry about money, debt, health care, and retirement is no small blessing for many and can come only when all are really treated equally. Now there's something to think about before you die.

In general, nuns also don't care at all about who makes the most money, has the most prestigious job, is the smartest, skinniest, or most attractive. Nor do they believe the one who dies with the most things wins. Nuns always have taken clear and consistent exception to all the ways this world calls women and men to be so preoccupied with competing and outdoing one another. Taking such clear and consistent exceptions yourself is something else to think about very seriously before you die. Imagine a world without winning and losing. Imagine a world without too much care about how you look or what you wear. Go ahead. Imagine a world.

A big part of being treated equal has to do with the belief that what binds people together is infi-

nitely more important than what sets them apart. Commonalities are treasured more than differences, which can be a blessing as well as a curse. Tendencies toward thoughtless or forced conformity should always be held suspect. The trick is to let the commonalities bind us together peacefully while letting the differences delight us, enrich us, educate us, and keep us alive.

Treating all equally is so important to nuns that it was made into a vow and called poverty. Contrary to popular opinion, poverty is not about how much money nuns do or don't make. It is about lifestyle and what you do with what you receive. Traditionally, regardless of how much nuns earn, it all goes into a common fund from which each sister gets the money she needs. Nontraditionally, nuns who are self-supporting and taxpaying care for one another in similar ways as well. Keeping too much is always discouraged. The secret lies in finding out how rich and abundant a simple life can be.

Nun or not, I highly recommend vowing some kind of poverty before you die, especially if you have more than enough with lots left over. Jesus reportedly asked that we give away what we don't truly need, or start stuffing ourselves through the eye of a needle. That's how hard it is to live a heavenly life with too much stuff. So take your pick. Share your surplus now. Or start stuffing yourself through the eye of that needle.

2. Nuns aren't interested in being married.

In a world that still holds single women suspect, I was delighted to grow up knowing groups of them who weren't interested in being married. So much so they made a vow of it. They were a strange, random mix of single women, joined together to do good work, to pray, and to preserve the solitary and communal life of the sisterhood. An oddity in every age and in every society, and for hundreds of years a profoundly attractive alternative as well—even if only for a minority of women.

The otherworldly ways of nuns were not entirely strange to me at the start, mostly because they held as sacred a kind of independence and freedom I knew and loved but barely understood. The idea of belonging to another person now or forever rarely appealed to me, though the basic idea of belonging always has. Being owned was something I never wanted to be either, and the very best way to prevent being owned is to remain unwed. Even the most primitive concepts of liberty involve the right to do what you want until you marry. Well, for nuns there were no untils. Being able to come and go as called is a holy rule of life. There's no being a good sister without it.

Because nuns were single, unmarried, unattached, and childless, there was always a very real sense in which they belonged to everyone. A very real sense in which nuns naturally became a sister to one and all. And being a good sister, as we all know, has far less to do with looking like a good nun should than it does with caring, understanding, and loving like a good nun should.

So while poverty teaches nuns how to treat one another equally, a life of celibacy teaches nuns how to love one another equally, as sisters and brothers. And when it comes to loving equally, nuns firmly believe that possessing, heavily depending on, isolating, and consuming inordinate amounts of time and energy are rarely good ways—not in the sisterhood or anywhere else. Those who bear divinity in their own right don't need approval from others. So anyone who lives their life in order to please others, be accepted, gain power, be liked, and win another's interest and love is no virgin. Now you can see why getting insight and depth would be critical developmental tasks for nuns—there's no being a virgin without them.

The unmarried part of a nun's life is always far more a matter of freedom to come and go as the Gods call than it ever is the lonely consequence of no lover, husband, or children. As any nun will tell you, sisterhood provides an incredibly rich and totally unpredictable life, with sisterly friendships as extraordinary as they are everlasting. And while you may never choose to live either a solitary or a celibate life, I suggest that you at least think about the kind of love life celibacy offers, and maybe even taste and see a little for yourself how sweet a life it really can be.

So there you have it. Nuns aren't interested in being married because the solitary life is their call. It preserves the loving sisterhood of women, fills life with mysterious and incredible events, generates infinitely compassionate lives and works, and, last, but not least, saves us all from the devastating

SIGN ON CONVENT DOOR

ILLUSTRATED BY ELLEN SEREMET, AT AGE 6.

effects of having and being had. Now you tell me, who in their right mind wouldn't want that before they die?

3. Nuns listen to God more than anyone else.

When it comes to decisions that affect their lives and work, nuns vow to listen to God before doing anything else. In taking a vow of obedience, nuns promise to listen to God first, then to one another. There's a discerning of Spirits that goes on whenever a group of believers listen to God all at once. The community voice, the voice all hear in common, helps filter out personal interference and misguided interests. So when nuns discern (alone and together) what the Gods are asking, it usually becomes pretty clear what's really divine and what's merely self-interest in disguise. Under the best of circumstances, what often emerges is a kind of common sense experienced as divine. Such listening is a high holy tradition in the sisterhood. Being a good sister depends on it.

Weighing pros and cons alone and together is a mysterious, incredibly reliable way for everyone to figure out God's will. Such simple discernment can help you see what you might not want to see and help you understand and accept perspectives much different from your own. It also helps prevent massive God abuse—the making of Gods in our own image and likeness. Mostly it just saves us from plain old ordinary stupidity. Something well worth being saved from every day before we die.

The work that nuns did—traditionally the church's work of teaching and nursing—also had a lot to do with obedience, with listening to God more than anyone else. Just as nuns revered as holy a woman's need for sisterhood and solitude, so too did they hold as sacred a woman's right and need to work. Nuns were career women long before the birth of modern feminism. But unlike most, nuns didn't apply for or get jobs. Instead, they "received obediences," assignments of what work they would do for the community. Such "obediences" included a wide range of activities—everything from teaching, nursing, even praying, to serving meals, scrubbing pots and pans, or pulling weeds out of the cracks of the sidewalk. Such "obediences" all represented God's work for you at the time, and all were to be accepted in that Holy Spirit.

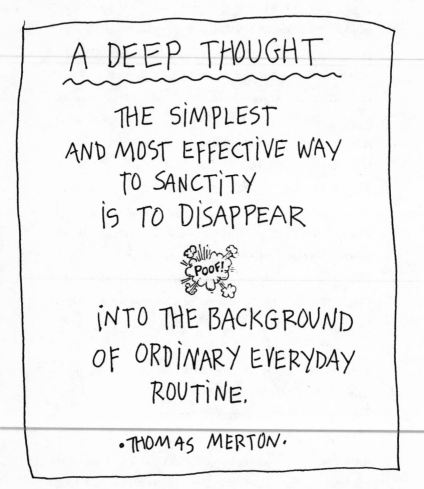

A DEEP THOUGHT

THE SIMPLEST
AND MOST EFFECTIVE WAY
TO SANCTITY
IS TO DISAPPEAR

POOF!

INTO THE BACKGROUND
OF ORDINARY EVERYDAY
ROUTINE.

· THOMAS MERTON ·

At first I wondered if we were led to believe that everything was God's work just in order to make the ridiculous more sublime. Most wouldn't dare complain and whine to the Gods over such minor matters as scrubbing showers and toilets. Even so, I always shared a secret bond with Saint Teresa of Avila, who complained to God after being thrown from her horse into a puddle of mud: "If this is how you treat your friends, it's no wonder you have so few of them."

Nonetheless, we did grow to believe that every situation and all work was holy, a quite ordinary way for us to experience daily the presence of God. We were taught to lay our hands on the ordinary things of life just as if they were all God's work, just as if they were the most divine works we could be doing. The most sublime as well as the most ridiculous, all is God's work. That is a mystical rule of life for nuns still.

All of us are born with some pure instinct, some call of the Gods to live our lives in a certain way, some call to do what we're put on this earth to do. There's a kind of psychic disposition in all of us that naturally turns toward experiencing how divine life can be. And somewhere in the turning lies the secret of who we are and what we're called to do. In listening to God more than anyone else, three things will happen: The secret of your life will be revealed bit by bit, you will be led to what's good for you, and you will always be given the courage and strength to follow.

Before you die, I strongly urge you to listen to the Gods more than anyone else, especially if you're dying to live happily ever after. Vow some kind of obedience to what your heart loves most, to whatever moves you deeply and offers you peace. Only then can you ever hope to taste and see how divine life can be, a joy not found separate or apart from this life but in the fullness of it. Such holy obedience is the source of your brilliance, the secret to your happiness, and the wellspring of your everlasting life. So before you die, make it your habit to listen to God more than anyone else.

A Word About Holy Disobedience

The hardest part of listening to God more than anyone else comes when the voice of God demands something different from the voice of authority, particularly religious authority. How regrettable that we are so poorly educated about what to do when the voice of God calls for noncompliance on our part. Instead we are taught that it is nearly sacrilegious even to suggest that the voice of authority might not represent the will of the Gods. The old killer instincts to strike dead all that challenge authority still haunt us, and fear of widespread insubordination still rules. Whether we ever need to be or not, we should at least know how to be conscientious objectors.

Before you die, give some serious thought to vowing holy disobedience whenever necessary. Discerning and knowing why one would choose to disobey is by far the most serious and mysterious part of listening to the voice of the Gods. It's also a recurring theme throughout the Bible. Biblical stories tell of four extraordinary circumstances that call for divinely inspired disobedience: the situation is unbearable and survival is at stake; the call to disobey promises deliverance; acts of disobedience would relieve oppression; and last but not least, swift, immediate divine intervention is not at all likely.

The only divine reasons for disobedience are

those that come from God and contain the moral imperative to set yourself and others free. In the end, holy obedience and holy disobedience appear as one and the same call—and both are held together by listening to the Gods more than anyone else. Given the sad shape of authority in this world, it's not a bad practice for everyone to vow before they die. What a cosmic event it would be if all humankind listened to the Gods more than anyone else. I imagine the whole world would be assumed into heaven. Or you could just assume that would be heaven. Whatever.

So there you have it: three perfectly good reasons to think about living like a nun before you die. After all is said and done, I urge you strongly to vow some kind of simple life in order to promote equality; some kind of solitude, possibly celibacy, in order to enrich your love life; and some kind of obedience (or holy disobedience) in order to bring your life together with your heart's desire. If well lived, a nun's life, like any well-lived life, is clearly more wonderful than all that can be said of it and really deserves to be thought about before you die—especially if all you think it means is none of this, none of that, and you'll never get picked to be one.

WHAT I ASPIRED
TO BE
AND WAS NOT
COMFORTS ME.

ROBERT
BROWNING

Seventh Thing:

Make
Yourself
Interesting

Making yourself interesting, as you may or may not recall, is one of the four main ingredients to having more fun than anyone else—which is number one on this list of things to do before you die. The absolute importance of making yourself interesting can never be understated for two big reasons: first, it has everything to do with not wasting your life, and second, it can be done only by you. If your everyday life feels boring, don't blame life, blame yourself. You and only you can make your life interesting.

Sometimes I think the most tragic human flaw lies in the slothful, sluggish belief that some of us automatically grow up interesting and others don't. Some get the fascinating gene and others get the blah gene. Wrong wrong wrong. No one automatically grows up anything. Being an interesting person is a big responsibility for us all, demanding steady, sometimes constant, effort.

Even though it may feel like hard work in the beginning, don't ever stop trying to make yourself interesting. Keep at it. Make it another daily habit in your secret life as a nun. Any effort to do so automatically prevents ending up good for nothing. Any attempt to make yourself interesting keeps you from wasting your life, which is the absolute worst thing you could ever do before you die.

With an infinite number of ways to make yourself interesting, it once again took me nearly half a century to find four:

Four Ways to Make Yourself Interesting

1. Cultivate a diverse group of friends.

What better way to make yourself interesting than to surround yourself with those different from and more interesting than you. All of that interesting energy can really rub off and inspire you, motivate you to become more interesting yourself. Remember, it's our differences that enrich us, delight us, educate us, and keep us alive. Surrounding yourself with a diverse group of friends will do all those things for you before you die, and more.

Associating only with our own kind, to the exclusion of everyone else, always brings out our worst features, our worst selves, and every hidden tendency we have to feel ourselves better than anyone else. All that exclusive familiarity inevitably breeds contempt, killing everything interesting about us, slowly but surely turning us into mean, hateful persons—wolves dressed in sheep's clothing. That's how deadly discrimination is to humankind. So don't be that way. It's hurtful, it's hateful, and it's so unnecessary. Do not do to others what you would not like done to you. It's that simple. And it's that holy and golden a rule.

Take a quick look now at your circle of friends. If all tend to be just like you, you all could be well on the road to a boring, wasteful, sorry life. Don't let that happen. On the other hand, if your circle of friends looks more like the United Nations assembled or any New York City jury pool, chances are your life will be increasingly jam-packed and fun-filled. So cultivate a diverse group of friends before you die. Not only will it make you infinitely more interesting as a result, but believe it or not, it will also help save the world as well.

2. Work.

Finding your best work is the third of the three biggest finds in your life—the other two being your best self and God. All three make up your life and cannot survive one apart from the other. Your very best God calls your very best self to your very best work. That's all there is to it. Your best work of art is always what you do with your life, not what life ends up doing with you. And it's the work that often rises from some necessity that always makes us more interesting.

The kind of work that makes you interesting has nothing to do with how much it pays or what title it gives you. That's not what makes you interesting. It may do other nice things for you, but it does not automatically make you interesting. Our real work

before we die is to find out what does make us interesting, what most sparks our interest. One of the
greatest responsibilities we all get at birth is that of
finding our life's work, finding out all along the way
what makes our life work best. In the heart of our
soul, we all need to find the work that lets us live
happily ever after.

Any work can become a work of art if we put
our best self into it. Best selves are always the magic
ingredient, the spark of genius in any work. Without
our best effort, whatever we do becomes boring,
stressful, numbing to mind, body, and soul.
Sometimes so much so it may give you a headache
or just make you sick. Having your best work mini-
mized or ignored will do the same. Whatever sparks
your interest will never make you sick like that. On
the contrary, you will rarely feel better. Headaches
and sickness from work are always clear signs to
pack up, go, and be not afraid. They're the loudest
and clearest calls we ever get to do something else
that would be far better for our health. Doing anything that makes you sick is never ever a virtue.

Before you die you must give some soulful
attention to what most sparks your interest. Find

TO
LOVE
WHAT
YOU
DO
AND
FEEL
THAT
IT
MATTERS --
HOW
COULD
ANYTHING
BE
MORE
FUN.

KATHARINE
GRAHAM

out what it is you want to do more than anything else. It could be parenting, gardening, teaching, building, writing. In a lifetime it could be all five, and more. Just follow the spark of your interest wherever it goes. That's one of the biggest secrets to everlasting life. It's also the singular most interesting thing you can ever do before you die.

3. Educate yourself.

In the context of making yourself interesting, education oftentimes has less to do with all the schooling you've finished and more to do with what you learn from life, from what each day offers. The worst thing you can ever do to yourself and others is feel completely educated after grade school, high school, years of college, or degree of degrees. The very minute you lose interest in learning something new every day is the very minute you start becoming ignorant. Something you never want to be before you die. You and the whole world suffer as a result.

I can write a litany of ways to educate yourself— all of which can easily fit into a day of your life. Read. Volunteer. See art and plays. Travel if you can. See the world. Spend time in galleries, museums, and libraries. Take a class. Meditate. A visit to any shopping mall is always an education. Make your own Litany of Higher Education before you die. Keeping yourself interesting depends on it. Without continuing your education, you increasingly run the risk of slowly but surely having less and less to say. You could easily end up grunting and groaning your way into old age. Never a very pretty picture. Always a sign of sad, wasted life. And reason enough, I hope, for you to continue to educate yourself until the day you die. Why have all that life in you and never use it? Don't die dumb like that.

4. Take sides.

Taking sides is no minor matter and has everything to do with your becoming as brave a soul as you are interesting. Taking sides gives the interesting person an even more interesting edge. Not only does taking sides make you exceptionally interesting, but it too actually can help save the world. In 1986 Elie Wiesel accepted the Nobel Peace Prize, pleading with us to "Take sides. Neutrality helps the oppressor never the victim. Silence encourages the tormentor never the tormented." He even made the

New York Times "Quotation of the Day" with those words. Makes you wonder very seriously if silence and neutrality are ever the virtues they're cracked up to be. History repeatedly shows us how extremely brutal, cruel, and deadly such neutrality can be—always far more than we'll ever know. Clearly and with great urgency, taking sides is one of the big virtues to be cultivated before you die. Not only will your life be immediately and always interesting as a result, but you also can really, truly help save the world as well.

One important thing to keep in mind when taking sides is to pick your battles carefully. Taking sides on every little thing does nothing but turn you into a royal pain in the neck—the person everyone loves to hate. Turning everything into a battle completely misses the whole point of taking sides—which is to have a point. Never take sides on the pointless. Take sides only on the important stuff, the stuff that touches your best self, your best God, and your very strongest beliefs. The right time for silence and neutrality comes only after consistently doing all you can. An incredible peace of mind also comes then, one of the most divine consequences of taking sides.

The most interesting, admirable, and enjoyable ones are always those brave enough to take sides. The most boring, deceptive, and sneaky ones usually are those who believe their divinely appointed role in life is to keep the peace. Avoid conflict. Make nice. Get crowned Miss Congeniality. Mr. Popularity. Never ever dare to take sides. The Book of Revelation clearly spells out their fate. So lukewarm and so sickening are they that God spits them out of his mouth. Ptooey. Ptooey. Ptooey. Something you don't want to happen to you before or after you die.

I hope you can now see that making yourself interesting takes considerable thought and effort and is exceedingly important to do every day before you die. The divine diversity of your friends, your work, and your education will surely do it for you, as will your habit of taking sides. So start now, if you haven't done so already. Make yourself interesting. I sincerely doubt that you want to risk ending up like one of those who make the Gods vomit.

Eighth Thing:

Live
Alone
for a
While

Without a doubt, living alone is one of the best things I ever did before I die; so much so I made a life of it, and in my heart a vow of it. My introduction to the solitary life also happened on day one of becoming a nun. Even before I found out we couldn't talk, I was given a room of my own. An eight-by-ten piece of solitude with bed, desk, bookcase, sink, closet, and, most important of all, window. We all got a room with a view. All ours was a piece of solitary splendor with sky. Little did I know at the time what a sweet mystery I found at last.

It took nearly twenty-five years, but that solitary room of my own gradually grew into the solitary life of my own—making it a magic ingredient on my list of things to do before you die. A defining point and a turning point for me, as it will be for you if given half a chance. Early in your adult life you must, if you can, live alone for a while—especially before you get married, live with someone else forever, or become a nun. There are things you need to find out about yourself before you live forever with someone else. You must find and get to know yourself first. It's too hard, sometimes impossible, to do later. Living alone for a while is a saving grace in any relationship as well as one big secret to living happily ever after.

In an attempt to help dispel some of the myths and fears about living a solitary life, I made a list of The Four Best and Worst Parts of Living Alone. My hope is that you'll start thinking about it so much that it will become for you a dream come true. I really know whereof I speak when I tell you that you never know at the start where living alone for a while will lead.

The Best Parts of Living Alone

1. Finding peace and quiet.

The peace and quiet dimension of living alone is clearly one of its finest, most divine features, always providing instant relief. There's nothing quite like coming home after a busy, noisy day to absolute peace and quiet. And nothing quite like waking up to the same. Thanks to answering machines and similar protective devices, you never even have to answer the phone. Any day can be a day of retreat, and every night can be one of Grand Silence. How great is that.

By affording you the luxury to withdraw completely from the constant demands of the day, living alone offers immediate gratification when it comes to peace and quiet. Only the still, small voice of your best self and God remains—the sound of which carries an inner peace and quiet all its own. You must know both kinds of peace and quiet before you die—inside and out. Waking up and coming home to both is clearly one of the very best parts of living alone.

2. Hearing voices other than your own.

While viewed by some as another sign of mental illness, hearing voices, like escaping reality, is clearly one of the best parts of living alone. Repeatedly the Bible shows us that God will not speak to us unless we're all alone. Until we go out into the desert or up to the mountaintop, God remains silent. Unless we slip away to some solitary place for a while, unless we go to our rooms and shut ourselves in, God is not likely to speak. Only when we're alone at last can we really hear with both inner and outer ears. That's the real truth of the matter. With all due respect to how difficult it is for us to listen, God knows that the chances of getting the message through to us are far greater when we're alone.

By virtue of its solitary splendor, living alone gives the Gods and their Muses unlimited and undivided access to our lives. We are all theirs, they are all ours, and therein lies the magic. Day by day, bit by bit, hidden mysteries of life become clearer. Living alone provides a gold mine of opportunity to find out everything about yourself: the kind of life you want to live, the kind of work you love to do, the kind of hospitality you want to offer, how late you want to stay up and how late you want to sleep, how strong you like your coffee, and so on. Living alone even allows you the freedom to be a hermit in a high-rise if that's the call you hear.

Whenever you need to get in touch with the Gods and Muses, I guarantee you can hear their voices more clearly in solitude. To that end, I suggest strongly that you make solitude a near and dear companion before you die. It's the only way we can hear the voice of God clearly. One of the very best parts of living alone is all the peace, quiet, and solitude it offers. All three are music to the ears of deities, moving them to speak, and us to listen. Always the makings for some enchanted evening.

3. Finding your very best self.

For those who live alone, it's no big surprise that the one person you'll always find at home is yourself. As long as you live alone you always have yourself to come home to. And on any given day there's always a lot more to be found there than at first meets the eye. Living alone gives you your life just as it is at the end of the day—for better or worse, in sickness and in health, sad, glad, mad, or bad. In living alone we always find ourselves just as we are, and learn, I hope, to know and love what we find. It's all the star stuff of life, and every bit of it is holy.

One of humanity's least attractive features is the tendency to blame its misery on someone else. Usually the nearest and dearest become targets. But in living alone the nearest and dearest is always yourself, so you learn quickly to deal with misery differently. You learn not to blame. If everyday life stinks, don't blame life, and don't even blame the stinkers. Most important of all, don't blame yourself. Don't blame anyone. Don't blame, period.

There is no good at all to be found in multiplying and spreading misery by taking it out on others. People get hurt and killed doing that. Too much of it and you quickly earn the reputation of being a hopelessly miserable person. Definitely something you do not want to be before or after you die. When misery strikes, do something other than spreading it around or taking it out on others. Try letting it be for a while. Leave it alone. It won't kill you. Nor will it last forever. If you need to do something with a bad day, try just letting it be.

The best advice to offer now and forever is to

BLESSED SISTER, HOLY MOTHER,
TEACH US TO CARE AND NOT TO CARE
TEACH US TO SIT STILL.
T.S. ELIOT

welcome and pay careful attention to whatever life gives you. Meeting your cares and woes day by day is far less disturbing in the long run than forever ignoring what they are, where they come from, and what to do with them. Too much of that kind of ignorance and you're really in trouble of dying clueless. Feeling miserable has yet to cause the end of the world even if that's exactly how it feels. However miserable we may sometimes find ourselves, living alone teaches us not to blame anyone at the end of the day. Not to blame, period. No more blaming, ever. Once we get that insight, once blame is gone from our life, the self we come home to every day will be found in a much happier, more peaceful state. Finding yourself like that is one of the most amazing graces there is and one of the very best parts of living alone.

4. Find new life.

Living alone can be as full or as empty of life as you make it. It's all up to you. There's no one at home to drain your energy but you. Pets and plants maybe, but ordinarily they're hardly ever an inordinate drain of energy. Once you get into the swing of living alone, it's not long before you begin to find all the kinds of new life and energy that solitude offers. It's not long before an eight-by-ten room of your own becomes a virtual fountain of youth on a mysterious island paradise. Well, that's a bit of an exaggeration, but you get the point. Living alone can be heavenly.

Sometimes solitude yields the perfect answer to a nagging problem. Sometimes keeping still and being quiet is part of the plan. Almost always you will find that solitude shows next steps and slightly alters your perspective. The outcome in any case is that a divine energy becomes available for life, a grace of sorts, sometimes extraordinary. New energy flows into life and important relationships, deepening and strengthening those bonds, even overflowing into all kinds of creative work, all kinds of pure fun.

One of the very best parts of living alone, now or forever, clearly lies in how faithfully solitude welcomes you home, gives you rest, carries you through, then lifts you up and returns you to life feeling pretty brand new. Now, that's my idea of a real good time.

The Worst Parts of Living Alone

1. It's hard work.

Because there's no one else at home to lend a hand with all the little things you have and hate to do, living alone means doing it all yourself. Pay bills, take down the trash (all separated for recycling), do laundry, clean house, floors, and windows, grocery shop, learn to fix things, mow the lawn, walk the dog, answer the phone and mail, set and dispose of mouse traps. Living alone is very high maintenance. And taking care of home and heart all by yourself is purely and simply a lot of work. Especially during unexpected crises like a Wednesday night at 9:24 when the living room ceiling falls on the living room floor.

The one magic ingredient that eases the burden of all that work in solitary is this: If it doesn't bother you, it doesn't need to be done. Yet. For those who care least about housekeeping, you really have to clean and make your bed only when company comes. And it's your responsibility to make sure that's often enough to prevent squalor. I feel about housework the way I feel about exercise: anathema.

While housework may be good, necessary, even divine for some, I hate it nonetheless.

Now, there are those who spend spare time cleaning bathroom tiles while loving every minute of it. Some actually enjoy all the hard work in living alone enough to spend weekends getting it done. I'm not one of them, nor do I know anyone who is. The thought alone makes me weak. Living alone always was and always will be hard work. I doubt that it'll ever be otherwise. It's absolutely the worst part of living a solitary life.

2. It's more stressful.

Practically everything written on stress these days shows how the load is greatest among those who live alone. No big surprise there. When it's just you and only you, it takes real effort to focus on something, anything other than yourself. When there's no husband, wife, children, or roommate to force your attention elsewhere, you are all you have to fall back on. In the immortal words of Lily Tomlin, "We're all in this alone." That in itself can be very stressful. A double whammy if you live alone.

Finding good ways to cope with all the excess

stress is probably one of the greatest challenges in living alone. While under- or overindulging any of our appetites only creates more stress, there's also nothing quite like good food, good drink, and good friends to make stress disappear. Meditation can do the same for you, as will that foaming, hot bath. It's in coping that you also draw on your experience with points one and four on this list: having fun and escaping reality. Draw on all the ways you know to take the day's load off and give yourself a rest.

3. It's sometimes lonely.

Living alone is sometimes lonely, and on occasion it can be terribly lonely. But then again, living in a group can be just as lonely, as can some marriages. Loneliness is a fact of life that has far less to do with living alone than it does with learning how to live, period. You've got to have friends. Finding good friends is one of life's greatest riches. It's entirely up to us to find lifelong friends and other ways of belonging that make any wave of loneliness entirely bearable.

If the loneliness you find in solitude always feels empty, maybe you need to fill it up some with the company of others. A life full only of your self is the source of most sad loneliness. And volunteering to help others can be a sure cure. It's the magic of being helped in helping others that you'll find filling. Dogs and cats are also known to have remarkable powers for filling the lonely lives of millions. If not being alone relieves some loneliness, then that's the call to follow.

Keep in mind that the loneliness you sometimes feel in living alone can be as sweet as it is sometimes sad. You will find that to be true also when you live alone for a while. The more you get a taste of the solitary life, the more you'll see how sweet and companionable living alone can be—and how amazingly full of grace.

4. It's more expensive.

The cruel fact that it always costs more to live alone is not fair and often becomes its most prohibitive and discouraging feature. There's nothing profound going on here. As a matter of fact there's probably less here than meets the eye. Paying for something yourself always costs more than sharing the expense. And initial household expenses are compounded further by the discriminating fact that no one throws showers for those who decide to live alone.

Not long ago I read about a woman who officially decided to remain single. She married herself in front of a mirror, minister, family, and friends. Because she had a big wedding she most likely had the benefit of a shower, but the majority who live alone never do. Everything it takes to make a house a home you buy yourself, and it's always a high price to pay. Too expensive is clearly one of the worst parts of living alone. Many can never afford it. But for those who can, the massive financial sacrifice is worth every last cent.

The Bottom Line

Well, now you can see that living alone is and isn't all it's cracked up to be. While finding peace and quiet, Gods and Muses, your self and new life, those who live alone also will find more work, more stress, sometimes more loneliness, and always more expense. Damned if you do, but even more damned if you don't. When it comes to living alone for a while, it's always far better to be damned if you do. So much so that living alone for a while should be required of everyone before we die, like a rite of initiation into adulthood—a definite must-do for all who want to live their lives with someone else forever.

For living-alone lifers, for those who decide to marry themselves, solitude easily becomes life's greatest joy and freedom. Not only are you able to do all ten things on this list whenever you want, but you also never have to worry about a whole host of tiny little important things, like staying too long in the tub, sharing the remote, the choice and volume of your music, even crumbs in the butter. No one cares if there are crumbs in your butter. No small bonus there.

CONVENT BUTTER

← NO CRUMBS.

KAROL JACKOWSKI'S BUTTER

← CRUMBS.

Ninth Thing:

Treat Yourself

When it comes to the care and feeding of your best self, there's no greater way to do both than by treating yourself, being good to yourself, taking care. Treating yourself is one of the first things to learn if you live alone, because if you don't, there's no one else around who will. No children, husband, or roommate to beg for favors. No one to manipulate into getting the ice cream, doughnuts, and pizza. No one to draw your bath. No one to bring you coffee and the morning paper in bed. No one to treat you in the way only you can. Who better than you knows what you want and when you want it. Learning to treat yourself is a must-do before you die. It has everything to do with loving yourself and being just as loving to others. Another big secret to everlasting life.

Now, for some the care and feeding of one's best self means lots of exercise, no meat, no fried foods, and no white flour or sugar. For others it means all of the above except exercise. Because I happen to be one of the others, the belief about treats promoted here is not at all exclusive, except of that which becomes excessive and harmful to body and soul. Moderation in all things, especially moderation. That's the rule when it comes to treating yourself.

Why Treat Yourself?

If you're wondering why it's so life-or-death important to treat yourself, just think about how hard life is sometimes. Therein lies your answer. Trying to be your best self, day in and day out, during the best and worst of times, is sometimes exceedingly difficult, and no one knows better than you the greatness of the difficulty. For that reason alone you should treat yourself often before you die. It's one way we have of sharing and enjoying the gifts of the

SISTER
SAYS:

MODERATION
is A
COLORLESS
INSIPID
THING
TO COUNSEL...
TO LIVE LESS
WOULD NOT
BE LIVING.

SISTER MADELEVA

Gods—among which are vanilla shakes, any day at the beach, fresh flowers in every room, a new book, home delivery of the *New York Times*, a trip to Stonehenge, a good margarita. Even a full-body gorilla suit can be someone's dream come true.

When it comes to treating yourself well, it's not hard for believers to be moved to treat others just as well. Treating others the way you treat yourself is a golden rule of life, assuming of course that you treat yourself exceptionally well. Mistreating, like misery, is not something you want to go around spreading. Nor should you ever tolerate any kind of mistreatment in your presence. Mistreating yourself and others is one of the absolute worst things you can do before you die. Don't do it at all. Don't even think of it. Get into the habit of treating yourself and others well instead. You deserve it. We all deserve it.

What Treats Do

The most important thing treating ourselves does is teach us how to treat others. Rule number one in most religions is always to do unto others as you would have them do unto you. Treat others the same way you want to be treated. It's all the same. By learning to care for and feed your very best self, you almost automatically learn how to care for and feed the very best selves of others.

In this regard, treating yourself is kind of magic, essentially religious, never merely self-indulgence. Love of neighbor is inseparable from love of self and God. Those who say they love God then turn around and hate a neighbor are big fat liars. Treating others as you would like others to treat you is one of the biggest lessons treats teach you. Make sure you know how to treat yourself and others well before you die. That too is the stuff of which final judgments are made.

The most divine part of all this treating can be found in how well we care about those we make out to be enemies—how endless our forgiveness is and how compassionate our forgetfulness. Treating ourselves shines most divine when it makes us patient, kind, not jealous, not snobbish, never rude, never moved to anger, with no limits on our trust, our hope, and our endurance—no limit to all those everlasting treats. May we all know what it's like to be well treated every day of our life. That's what living happily ever after looks like.

Tenth Thing:

Live Like You Have Nothing to Lose

Well now, if you've faithfully worked your way through all nine points so far, skipping none, the only thing left to do before you die is live like you have nothing to lose. With all the searching, digging, escaping, listening, losing, and finding that goes on in the first nine things, chances are you already have nothing left to lose. While point by point these ten things may appear innocent, harmless, and funny, they can in the end be real killers of our worst selves. One by one they get rid of the stuff that messes up our lives and makes us miserable, leaving us in the end with little or nothing to lose.

There is nothing worse in life than loss, especially if we have a lot to lose. Life doesn't get much more mysterious than it does when we experience loss. Losing those we love always feels like more than we can bear, giving us a taste of what dead feels like before it slips into new life. The hardest part of nothing left to lose always lies in the loss of absolutely everything. Even the fear of loss has to go. Everything.

Well, thanks be to the Gods for the cyclic movements of life. The waxing and waning of the moon. Winter turning into spring, summer into fall. Night turning into day, day into night. The universal beliefs about death and rebirth. Having lost all there was to lose, what remains is mysteriously not dead but secretly stirring with some kind of new life. While the dead of winter may look and feel that way, beneath the snow always lay the seeds of spring. Nature herself tells us that some kind of mysterious transformation always takes place with every loss we know. Regardless of how dead every kind of loss feels, new life lies hidden there. Just wait and see.

We all rise again like the moon. The Gods raise us all from the dead, but nothing like before. Always somehow more brand new. Surely more fearless. More indestructible. More accepting. Wiser. Funnier. Calmer. Capable of being assumed into heaven at any given moment. All such things are known to happen in the new life. All are signs of one newly risen from the dead.

With nothing left to lose, even the ordinary manner of life feels far less out of control and far more full of surprises. No longer so fearful of losing it all the time, life doesn't wear you out or make you mad and miserable anymore. Daily events no longer have that power over you. Even loss becomes part of the mystery of life, one of God's crooked lines. Perspective gets bigger and broader and compassion is felt for all who suffer. Your heart cannot help but go out to those in need. Even miracles are known to happen. Those too are signs of new and everlasting life.

Healing from any loss comes *slowly but surely, in its own and our best time*. We gradually regain consciousness—like dry bones do when they come back to life—and in doing so begin to find all that can never be lost or taken away. Peace becomes the gift of the Gods then, a peace that goes beyond understanding. Eventually dem dry bones get breath, flesh, skin, and come back to life again. And just as soon you will know more days than not that make you want to cry out for joy. A joy with nothing missing. That's the surest sign there is that you have nothing left to lose.

So now you can see that living with nothing to lose is the closest to heaven you can get. All parts of life gradually become noticeably more divine, noticeably more fun than ever before. Here too we have one of life's wildest mysteries—the end and the beginning running into each other over and over again like some kind of eternal life. Which is what these ten things aim to do for you before you die: show you how to undo misery and death and live forever. Not bad for ten bucks.

WHAT WE CALL THE BEGINNING IS OFTEN THE END
AND TO MAKE AN END IS TO MAKE A BEGINNING.
THE END IS WHERE WE START FROM.
                    T.S. ELIOT

AFTERWORD

At this point in the "Ten Things to Do Before You Die" lecture, there was a personal demonstration of living like you had nothing to lose. Pointing out that the demonstration could indeed be the last thing I did before I died, I also explained that no nun and dean at the age of forty-two should ever do what I was about to do unless there was clearly nothing left to lose. The students were given cinnamon lips candy and the assignment to think through the list and pick their favorite thing to do before they die. I disappeared briefly to prepare for the finale.

Five minutes later I appeared from the balcony and finished the lecture in a full-body gorilla suit—

something I always wanted to do, a dream come true. While a good time was clearly had by all, certainly I had more fun than anyone else. As you can probably guess, having more fun than anyone else, finding a place to escape reality, and treating yourself were top favorites among the students. While thinking about nuns was not, all admitted it was far more interesting than they ever thought possible. The other points were way too serious and way too heavy to think about on a starry starry spring night. While recognized as absolutely necessary and commendable, the remaining items received polite but not widely enthusiastic applause.

With regard to the whole list of ten things, all are advised to begin with and work through all ten, omitting none. That way you're sure to keep ending up at the beginning. Unable to lose and incapable of dying, you just keep getting better and better, closer and closer to being all that you can be. Life becomes more divine, and you become assumed more and more into heaven. Or you can just assume that's heaven. Whatever.

In the end this is just one list and one story. Once upon a time, there lived a girl who had more fun than anyone else, got some insight, got some depth, found a place to escape reality, wrote every day, thought about being a nun, made herself interesting, lived alone, treated herself, and lived like she had nothing to lose. She did all ten things before she died and lived happily ever after. For ten bucks you even get a fairy-tale ending.